MW01234537

Understanding Narcissism

A Life-Changing Guide To Escaping Narcissism & Narcissistic Personality Disorder

Written By

Hilary Parker

Table of Contents

INTRODUCTION

Thank you for purchasing this book!

Since powerful feelings are the most vigorously charged, a mystic empath frequently grabs and acclimatizes these. This isn't an issue if the empath is one who has a consistent positive frame of mind and a consistently upbeat and cheerful attitude. Such an individual will end up happy around other people who offer that proclivity, and no damage is finished.

Compassion regularly ends up tricky, in any case, for one who has encountered much affliction and battle throughout everyday life. Such an individual will, in general, get exceptionally adversely charged feelings or even physical side effects of people around them. They understand, similar to a magnet, the sentiments of others that mirror their own; and they will every now and again feel over-burden.

Empathic compassion is a blessing, not a revile; however, many would oppose this idea. Vitality healers, restorative intuitive, and otherworldly advisors regularly have this aptitude and use it in their day by day work. These people can frequently discharge the pessimistic energies from themselves and those they serve. At all, sympathy gives the expert a premise from which to coordinate the customer's recuperating procedure.

Enjoy your reading!

TYPES OF NARCISSISM

Though NPD is bunched together, there are three main ways narcissists present, with three very distinct patterns of behavior. Some narcissists are loud, rowdy, and unapologetically grandiose, true to the stereotypical narcissist. Others are much quieter and covert with their behaviors. Another subset altogether seems to exist solely to watch the world burn. Narcissism as a whole is generally toxic in some way or another to those around the narcissist, but they vary in how toxic they can be. This chapter will guide you through the defining features of the grandiose, vulnerable, and toxic narcissist.

The Grandiose Narcissist

This kind of narcissism is sometimes referred to as overt narcissism, and it consists of the stereotypical narcissist. If you are asked to identify or describe a narcissist, chances are, the kind of person you would describe is grandiose. These are the ones who wholeheartedly believe they are better than everyone else, and they will always act as such. They do not care what those around them think about them and hold the belief that anyone who does think badly about them is mistaken and their opinion is useless because of that.

These people genuinely have high self-esteem, even to the point of delusion. This self-esteem becomes the basis for the narcissist's belief that he is always right and superior. Even with the evidence in front of him saying otherwise, he will absolutely insist that he is right. Oftentimes, the grandiose narcissist is the product of a disjointed upbringing or a feeling of having things handed to him or her. He truly believes in his high self-esteem, even if it is unwarranted, oftentimes due to growing up in a setting that granted power or superiority. This could be someone who had some sort of natural talent that constantly put him at the top rank effortlessly, or it could be the result of growing up in a household that taught him that he was better than others. If he grew up hearing that he was better than others, special, unique, and given some sort of power, such as over a nanny or other domestic workers, he may internalize that voice and use it in all aspects of his life.

The grandiose narcissist will not hesitate to tell everyone every redeeming feature or success he has had if he thinks it may be admirable. He will gladly offer up the information about his most recent performance review at work or the grades on the latest midterm if he feels as though they reflect his superiority. Even if he has to embellish the situation to make him look good, he will not hesitate to do so. Oftentimes, this bragging also comes alongside putting down the listener's recent achievements in ways that bring the narcissist up a level.

In relationships, the grandiose narcissist does not care about his partner or his partner's opinion of him. The partner and anyone else with whom the narcissist forges a relationship is seen as a tool, and if he feels as though the tool has outlived its usefulness, he will not hesitate to toss it out and replace it with something he believes is better. If he still sees use in the relationship, he will do the absolute bare minimum to keep the partner around and willing to continue the relationship.

Grandiose narcissists are notorious for refusing to apologize. Even if there could be some benefit to apologizing, the grandiose narcissist will refuse, except for under very specific circumstances. To apologize is to admit fault and to admit inferiority, and he refuses to do so. The only time a grandiose narcissist is willing to apologize is when the person he has wronged in some way is superior.

Oftentimes, the grandiose narcissist engages in what is known as magical thinking, which essentially believes that whatever he thinks is true and that if he thinks it hard enough, he can make it happen. This is a sense of entitlement, and the narcissist wholeheartedly believes he deserves without effort. Pairing this entitlement with his infallibility and superiority, he truly believes there is no way he could not possibly get what he wants. The idea of not getting it is entirely inconceivable to him.

Despite this magical thinking, grandiose narcissists are the most flexible of the types of narcissists. He will always act in ways that will manipulate the situation, and even if things may not entirely go according to plan initially, he has no qualms with manipulating to regain favor and control over the situation. If he is unable to regain control and get what he wants, he somehow manages to convince himself that not getting what he wanted is actually what he wanted all along.

The Vulnerable Narcissist

In contrast to grandiose narcissists, vulnerable narcissists frequently avoid detection. They are more subtle, sometimes referred to as covert narcissists by other sources. Vulnerable narcissists are sensitive in general, especially to rejection, abandonment, and change, and due to their sensitivity, they often oscillate between feelings of superiority and inferiority, depending on their environment. During periods of inferiority, the vulnerable narcissist seeks validation from others in the form of narcissistic supply with the intention of boosting his or her ego.

Oftentimes, vulnerable narcissists are hiding low or nonexistent self-esteem. They often develop a victim persona with the sole purpose of earning sympathy and allowing for more manipulation of the situation around them. They always seek to make themselves innocent in all conflicts, preferring the victim role. The victim role either brings others running to the narcissist's rescue, feeding her ego, or causes her to be able to point blame and fault on other people, even if she did, in fact, cause the problem to begin with.

Despite the victim persona vulnerable narcissists well so well, hiding behind a meek and quiet demeanor, they are quick to explode when angered or challenged. The more vulnerable a narcissist is, the harsher they respond to any sort of direct challenge to her ego. She may first begin to use passive aggression, wording things just right in order to deny fault in the future, but if that does not work and she still does not get her way, she will resort to direct aggression.

Self-conscious, she constantly obsesses over her own appearances, attempting to overcompensate so other people will boost her ego, even if only temporarily. In contrast to grandiose narcissism, which is born from unrealistic expectations, vulnerable narcissism is typically the result of childhood trauma and poor relationships with early caregivers who were supposed to protect her. She uses narcissism as a way to shield from the feelings of worthlessness and being unlovable and craves the closeness and attachment to others that she may have been denied as a child.

Because she cares about appearances, the vulnerable narcissist will seek to build rapport with others in any way possible, if she values that particular relationship. She still lacks some degree of empathy, but she is willing to apologize when necessary and recognizes how her behaviors impact those around her. Despite being more in-tune with others' feelings, she will still only act in ways that benefit her. She will engage in good deeds, but only if someone is present to witness. She strives to be someone that everyone looks up to, but only wants to be that person when eyes are on her.

The Malignant Narcissist

Both vulnerable and grandiose narcissism essentially show the inverse of each other. One involves inflated self-esteem while the other involves a lack of stable self-esteem. Neither of these is particularly toxic if the narcissist is not actively going out of his way to harm others. However, one kind of narcissist loves to harm others, going out of his way to intentionally create this sort of toxicity. Malignant narcissists thrive on chaos, loving the act of causing pain anywhere they go and thriving on the reactions earned.

The malignant narcissist frequently combines NPD with tendencies of sadism and paranoia, both of which are hallmark features of antisocial personality disorder. This combination creates a monster who revels in pain while still desiring to be the center of attention at all times. Lacking empathy, he has no reason to stop what he is doing when people are being harmed. He craves attention, even if that attention is negative, and if wreaking havoc is the easiest way to get massive amounts of attention, then so be it.

When attention is removed from the malignant narcissist, he will likely stir up trouble in some way simply because then at least people are acknowledging him, even if it is negatively. Without the desire to be admired by others, he has no issues with being the heart of chaos. Along with his antisocial tendencies, the malignant narcissist blatantly disregards the law and other social norms. He will lie just because he can with no regard for the consequence, feeling as though the laws are irrelevant to him due to his own superiority complex. Sometimes, the malignant narcissist will even pick up violent tendencies, resorting to terroristic behaviors or becoming serial killers. By having the ability to harm others, the narcissist feels as though he affirms his own superiority and importance.

When not causing trouble, malignant narcissists frequently appear charming, using their manipulation skills and perfected mask of charisma in order to gain trust. They are also quick to seek out physical intimacy, though it is meaningless to the narcissist. They see the intimacy as a tool, recognizing that it will keep their newest target more interested for longer in maintaining the relationship, even with all of the bad parts. Intimacy also becomes a weapon, with the malignant narcissist withholding it whenever it suits him best. The malignant narcissist recognizes that, for the average person, intimacy is used to increase bonding and deepening the relationship.

As a natural manipulator, the malignant narcissist always seeks out anything he wants, with no qualms about manipulating other people to get it. Between his lack of empathy, his flagrant disregard for social conventions and laws, and his sense of entitlement and superiority, he creates a monster that is hardly recognizable as human. These people should be avoided, as sometimes, they hurt others just because they can, with no provocation and no reason.

HOW TO RECOGNIZE A NARCISSISTIC MOTHER?

The below list is a compilation of the key characteristics a narcissist displays, specifically narcissistic mothers. If you want to be sure that either your mother or someone else's is a narcissist, then study and consider the below list:

Common Traits of Narcissistic Mothers

She Is Unable to Be Empathetic

Narcissists are sometimes able to form bonds with others, whether we're talking about a love interest, a friend, or their own offspring. However, those bonds are not what you might expect.

When most people connect with others, that connection is based on understanding and mutual benefit. These are healthy relationships that have their highs and lows, but in most cases both sides share rights and responsibilities.

Narcissists however lack the ability to empathize. They sincerely can't put themselves in your shoes and give compassionate care. A narcissistic mother has no insight about her demeanor and she can't understand or empathize with other people. She can pretend briefly but is defined by her lack of empathy. Most people will approach a situation with some empathy. They try to experience others' feelings or opinions from their perspective. This may not always be achieved of course, but most people at least try. Empathy means that we "step outside of our own agendas long enough to develop an understanding of the other person's perspective".

You can't have a truly reciprocal relationship without this happening on both sides.

She Is Exploitive & Manipulative

She never spares anyone's feelings, but she makes sure that you would feel extra guilty if you don't spare hers. She is amazing at manipulation, and you walk away from every conversation wondering how you came around to agreeing with her, despite your determination not to. She will control and manage interactions between others, much as a 'puppet-master' behind the scenes. She is a master at this, but so subtle that it is often incredibly hard to pin down what is happening. When she fights, she fights to win. She doesn't care who she has to hurt, or how much, in order to win an argument.

She Has A Strong Sense of Entitlement

She sincerely believes that she deserves the best; more than others deserve in fact. She is entitled to the best, at least in her mind and the personal 'reality' she has created. She has an entitled assumption that others should be doing things for her, helping her, and fixing things for her. For some reason she believes this is what the world owes her. She takes no responsibility for her mistakes or issues, but instead believes others should save her from them.

She Will Embarrass You in Front Of Others

She will bring up embarrassing stories about you in public. She will humiliate you repeatedly in this way, but make it appear that it is all a joke; maybe even a family joke or story that is often told. However, she will save these moments of cruel 'teasing' for when in public.

She Is Unable to Receive Direction

Narcissists are completely unable to take direction or correction. It just doesn't register. Well, the fact that you are giving them feedback will register (and you will suffer for it), but any consideration of possibly taking that feedback on will not register.

She can't handle even the smallest amount of criticism. She is perfect just the way she is, and everyone else is just jealous.

She Has an Insatiable Need for Control

Regarding control, Carter states that "the strong craving for control in narcissists typically grows out of a disordered sense of power dynamics". In childhood, one or both parents were generally "overbearing or heavy-handed in dealing with anyone who dared to disagree with them".

Remember, they are inherently a very injured person. Being in control feels safe to them. Of course, if they lost control of everyone around them, nothing bad would happen, but it's impossible to convince them of this, as to feel out of control is what a narcissist fear most.

She Is Judgmental & Thinks She Is Better Than Others

As far as achievements go, she doesn't really need to have any. She can easily feel superior to everyone else without having achieved anything. If she has achievements, she will use this to always keep her platform of superiority and control.

She Refuses to Acknowledge Reality

She creates her own reality, and what is even scarier, she sincerely believes it. She will recount situations completely differently to how they actually happened. Her 'spin' on events is often a masterful twisting of the truth. Look out for often repeated phrases like, 'I'm just saying it like it is', or 'I'm just being honest'. When significant events occur in her life, or in the lives of others around her (e.g. bereavement, redundancy, divorce), she will often refuse to truly acknowledge them, or their true impact and consequences. She will also somehow make all these situations about her.

She Is Able To Create Very Favorable Public Impressions

Most narcissists are very good at convincing people that it's everyone else who is the problem or defective, never them. They are charming, often good at talking, and incredibly convincing and persuasive.

As far as other people are concerned, you have the perfect parents; they love you, care for you, and do everything for you. If you have anything bad to say (or even think) about the situation, then you're an ungrateful little brat. The worst part is that even though you know in your heart that's not true, you still feel this way. Although she trivializes your achievements, that won't stop her from bragging to her friends. However, she's not doing it because she's proud of you, but because she wants everyone to know what a wonderful mother she is.

She Lacks the Ability To 'Self-Reflect'

When someone is truly a narcissist, it is incredibly rare that there is ever any change, as they are incapable of true self-reflection. Self-reflection would expose them as wrong and a narcissist can never be wrong. To be wrong in their opinion is to be flawed, and they cannot ever be seen as flawed. Most of the time your mother has no idea why she does what she does, which can make her quite destructive.

Narcissists are notorious for ignoring their problems, so don't even start to think that you can change your mother. You can't even help her see that she has a problem. She has some enormous 'blind spots', that she will do anything to avoid seeing. The best thing you can do is damage control, not for her, but for you.

Everything is always about her.

No conversation happens without her talking about herself, or making other people talk about her and admire her. This leaves the child feeling non-existent.

She Constantly Trivializes Other's Achievements.

Other's achievements are always trivial to her, no matter how grand they actually are. This is particularly true of her children, and others in her life who may be a threat to her.

She Has a Short Fuse, known as 'Narcissistic Rage'

She is easily angered, frustrated and disappointed. This leaves everyone 'walking on eggshells' around her, always trying to keep her in her charming phase, and not snapping into her angry and vindictive self. However, she is unpredictable, and the smallest thing can set her off; spiraling into narcissistic rage.

Narcissistic Rage is an essential characteristic for the child of a narcissistic to understand, as it is this that the child fears most. This can be both in the form of aggressive rage, or passive aggressive. However, the 'passive' stage is generally just simmering under the surface, ready to explode. It is another form of control; this keeps everyone in line. It is remarkable how quickly they will calm down from their drama once they have gotten what they want, and everyone else is quivering like jelly from the explosion (or the waiting for the explosion).

TREATMENT FOR CHILDREN OF NARCISSISTIC MOTHERS

The problem with narcissistic mothers is that they never feel attached to their baby, and so they are incapable of loving and cherishing their child. As you have learned by now, the narcissistic parent views their son or daughter as an object or property rather than a beloved individual. The narcissist mom will use her child to her advantage and see them as a nuisance to their lives. The child is then never seen for who they are, and their growth to become individuals becomes non-existent or slower than others. As a result of this type of childhood, the child grows up trying to fill the void or emptiness their parents didn't fill through unhealthy behaviors, such as developing NPD

themselves or abusing drugs and alcohol. Two paths lead the child to either becoming entitled like their narcissistic mother or trying to please everyone to fill the void of validation and acceptance. Both paths lead to unhappiness. The narcissism path may lead to success and power, but they are never happy because they are chasing validation and attention that only their mother can fill. The people pleaser struggles with a lifetime of approval from others, which can make them feel even more lonely and confused.

An Abusive Relationship

Children who grow up with a narcissistic parent often don't realize that they are being raised by a narcissist. They have this superior image of their parents, which follows the belief that their folks would never hurt them because they love them.

However, this type of belief can damage an adult because if they become people pleasers, they may end up in a narcissistic or abusive relationship. As it feels normal to them, they continue to the relationship and never grow into the person they need to be due to the never-ending 'normality' of abuse that surrounds their universe.

On the other hand, if the child ends up a narcissist themselves, they may endure an unhealthy relationship that competes for power and control over one another. Because their spouse isn't their mother, the child (who is now an adult) strives to be the very best and may end up abusing their partners because this is also 'normal' for them.

As every relationship starts out great, there is a honeymoon phase that you may go through with a potential lifetime partner.

However, being a narcissist yourself or having a narcissistic partner is just the beginning to a lifetime of unhappiness and deep-rooted emptiness. Whichever the conclusion is, there are a few manipulative behaviors that can be done from the abuser that you should know about before seeking out protection and treatment.

1. Publicly charming yet devilish behind closed doors Because of the narcissists image and reputation they need to uphold, they will charm you, cater to you, act kind and compassionate to you, etc. in public. But the minute you get home, they become the ultimate bully by lashing out at you for what your brother said to them that was insulting or how you behaved at the restaurant.

2. Have a fixated self-image while sabotaging yours Narcissists are pathological liars. What this means is that they exaggerate their experiences and achievements so that people will see them as superior and worthy. They tell individuals what they want them to believe to either take pity on them or see them as a higher up individual. Meanwhile, as much as they lie about their experiences and exaggerate, they will also undermine all your achievements,

especially if they aren't lies. This is because they think anyone they see is better than them and feel entitled to being better than you. When you have accomplished something, they may shrug it off like no big deal, take your spotlight, or take credit for your achievements by saying they put you where you are.

3. Superior and sensitive

The biggest fear that a narcissist will suffer with is knowing that someone will see their flaws, especially in public. Due to these fears, the narcissist will rarely say sorry or feel as though they have done anything wrong. When they are called out, they play the victim card and blame their loved ones.

4   Entitled and depriving

A narcissist's self-centered nature makes them feel entitled to getting what they want no matter how they get it. Yet when it comes to your needs and approval, they give it out sparingly. The narcissist will undermine anyone else's experiences, such as if their spouse came home and cried due to getting fired, but they compete with it by ranting off someone or cutting in front of them.

5   Offensive and defensive

The vulnerable narcissist will be passive-aggressive with their sarcastic insults or underlying compliments, whereas the malignant narcissist will intentionally pick fights to see how far they can push you. On the other hand, when they are questioned or criticized for their behavior, they are too quick to become defensive. The defensiveness may come out as a pity party for themselves or by gaslighting your experiences to make you doubt your conclusion.

6   Righteous and cold-hearted

A narcissist always needs to be right or know what comes next as a result of their perfectionism. They will plot, plan, clean, make permanent decisions, etc. When any of these details goes wrong or was misread, the narcissist will sink into despair or lash out in violent behavior.

7 Emotional yet non-empathetic

When a narcissist is upset, you will know. It is your job to make them feel better no matter which state you are in. Instead of trying to help you, though, they will put on a fake emotion to grab the attention from you and ensure that you are always pleasing them. This behavior stems from the lack of empathy and emotional intelligence.

Knowing these signs of an abusive or narcissistic relationship can help you define your future and seek recovery. The truth is, you cannot help a narcissist see the light or convince them to get help for their deep-rooted insecurities as they will deny it anyways. All you can do is seek protection and treatment for yourself. More importantly, if you see a child suffering from it, help them before it's too late (Neuharth, 2019).

How to Help a Child Who Suffers From Narcissistic Parenting Abuse

As you have learned, a child who is raised in a narcissistic home can be abused in multiple ways even when something is not their fault. For example, their mother might be fighting with a sibling or her spouse and lash out at her child as a way to make herself feel better. She may use her child as a pawn against her significant other or take advantage of them in a difficult situation. Co-parenting with a narcissist can be difficult because the moment you stand up and say something, the narcissistic parent may deny you food, shelter, money, and support. If they can't hurt you, they will find a way to hurt your child in a painful and shocking way.

Here are circumstances that may guide you in helping yourself and your child.

If your child is taken against you or away from you. The most painful experience to a parent is having their kid used against them in a fight or when the narcissist has the power to take the child away completely. If the act isn't painful enough, the sure threat of it can be debilitating.

One way a child may turn against you on their own will is if the narcissistic parent has planted ideas or thoughts into their head about you. Here is the hard truth: The more you become emotional, upset, depressed, or even angry, the more fuel you add to the fire. The more you fight back or defend yourself, the worse the situation may become. The solution to dealing with this type of matter is to accept and come to terms with who you are.

Only you know what you believe in and stand for. Ignore what has been done and said and don't try to convince your child that their other parent is narcissistic. Do not fight back or give the narcissist your emotional power because if you do; otherwise, you will end up like the narcissistic parent, which can be damaging and make you feel crazy. At the same time, do not resent your child for feeling the way they do as it is not their fault.

Instead, focus on your love and compassion for them. Take advantage of every moment spent with them, leaving the narcissistic parent out of all your conversations with them.

Answer honestly as well and be grateful for the time you get.

You have suspicions about your child becoming narcissistic It is important to take note of the fact that if your child has one non-narcissistic parent who sets healthy boundaries and influences them in any way they can. It is unlikely the child will become narcissistic. If there are already clear signs that your child may be becoming narcissistic, just envision them getting better. Focus on them becoming structured and responsible adults. Lastly, learn how to set positive and effective boundaries for yourself, as well as teach them boundaries of their own. You fear the narcissistic parent and their rights to your child. In this scenario, let's say that you have the child in your custody and the narcissistic parent has visitation rights or joint custody.

Focus on the facts here: you have the right to deny or withhold access to your child IF you suspect violence, abuse, or an unsafe situation for your child. However, it may be extremely difficult proving that your co-parent is a narcissist, especially because they are good at lying and faking in public situations. This doesn't mean you should give up trying to stop the abuse from happening. This circumstance is extremely difficult since your child may be caught in the middle if you decide to take action against the narcissistic parent. All that does is fuel their emotional fire and result in some extremely difficult time.

The best thing to do is to accept what's happening for what it is.

It won't be long until your child can make decisions for themselves; putting them through the stress of your baggage will only result in a damaged relationship. Let go of the power that the narcissist holds over you and find inner peace within yourself to help you cope through the challenging relationship. Only talk to them as needed and be one with your child when you are with them. Through these actions, your child will grow up knowing you did your best for them rather than bringing them into the drama. This will eventually allow them to make the right decision for themselves.

Your child is being abused in a narcissistic relationship. The first step is not to control your child or make them resent their partner. After all, it is up to them to learn through their own experiences. The second step is to be supportive and give them lots of empathy. As much as you believe that they deserve better, that they are smart, and talented, just know that unless you have endured a narcissistic relationship yourself, you can never understand the true power they can hold over someone. The truth is that the relationship isn't as simple as saying, "I am walking away." It's an addictive relationship in which your child is gaining some benefit as long as the narcissist continues to supply him or her with their needs and wants. If you try to persuade your child against their partner, they are going to endure the relationship more. They are the only people who can come to terms with the abuse and fix it themselves.

For this difficult and confusing time in your child's life, all you can do is support them and provide unconditional love. Show them respect and hope that one day they will realize what is happening. You can merely focus on your self-growth from this experience. Let go of the pain that is holding you back, release the worry deep within you, and visualize your child recovering and becoming well. When you put this type of energy into the universe, the universe will pay you back with loads of positivity.

Although this may be difficult for you to do, just remember that your child needs to suffer through this life lesson to grow into her or his own individual. When you practice the belief that things will turn out as they are supposed to and let the universe handle it, you can really help your child through this experience.

Essentially, the best way to help your child out of a narcissistic relationship of any kind is to first help and heal yourself. Once you have done this, you can offer your support and guidance during the process. Be there for them when they need to vent or cry or lash out.

Understand that strength comes from within, and you cannot guide

a troubled soul without first understanding and being able to let go

of your personal vindictiveness.

THE CONTINUING CYCLE

Especially when a narcissist knows that you are not willing to speak with them, they will have an ambassador in their place. This concept is known as sending out the Flying Monkeys. These people may or may not be aware of the situation or even that they are being used as a way to help the narcissist to get back into your life. You are in worse trouble if they are aware of their position as they most likely are another narcissist that will work you on another angle.

The main reason that narcissists end up chasing you is that they feel or think you have something that they want. This can be the case in reality or a fantasy in their minds.

Narcissists are also reluctant to let go over a former victim before they have successfully controlled another. This is where you will find there are overlaps in relationships with a narcissist. It is a safety net for them to have someone that they know they can gain the attention from a phone call away. Narcissists cannot stand being alone, and as such are always on the prowl.

Depending on the level of usefulness the narcissist has placed on their victim is the amount of energy they are going to input to acquire the new victim. If there is a low level of usefulness, they will put in little effort. However, if they feel the victim is invaluable, they will single-mindedly go after their goal with gusto.

When the victim finally takes the opportunity to leave the relationship, they may find that the narcissist is not able to let them go. They will start over with the manipulation process by starting to love bomb the ex or convince the victim that they are willing to change.

At this stage, it is possible for the narcissist to promise the moon if they feel they are of any value any longer. Victims must be careful during this tricky step. It is easy to fall back into the same patterns which will land them right back to the situation that they had left, but most likely, this time it will be worse. Remember that it never permanently gets better with a narcissist involved.

Even if the love bombing and honeymoon period lasted for months beforehand, do not think for one moment that this will happen again. It will likely be a month or less until the narcissist switches back to the manipulative and controlling partner.

Because of this fact, the times that the victim is able to escape from their personal hell need to be cherished and fully taken advantage of as each time you leave and come back, the honeymoon period will get shorter and shorter and they quickly remember the reasons why they left and probably have another reason to add to the list.

When the victim decides to leave and implement no contact, this drives the narcissist into hyperactive mode. They scramble to do anything and everything in their power to bring you back to them and thus bring control back to the narcissist. Since the victim is the narcissist's attention supply, the narcissist is left completely powerless while feeling worthless and small.

The psychological power shift from the narcissist to the victim is instantaneous when no contact is implemented, and the narcissist is unable to function as they have lost the power they have worked so hard to possess as well as the emotional punching bag.

A common misconception of victims is when the narcissist is changing their behavior to come back into their good graces to have a relationship again; they believe that the narcissist must love them.

This again is just repeating the cycle again because this is how the narcissist was able to catch the victim in the first place.

This is a very difficult part of the process in which the victim needs to remain strong. They must remember the reasons why they left the narcissist and stick to their guns. It is because the victims are usually still very much in love with the narcissists despite it all, and it is quite easy to run back into the arms of the familiar. This is especially the case if the narcissist had kept the victim isolated from the outside world for some time as the victim will have a hard time adjusting to everyday life again.

Yes, the victims know that the relationship was a negative thing for them and that they are walking straight back into the misery, but it is extremely easy to get drawn back in time and time again. Because they fell in love with the idea of a person that they could relate to, it is difficult to stop feeling those emotions when even a shimmer of the old partner shines through. It makes the victim believe yet again that they were right about there being something good inside this monster of who their love has become.

The real reason behind the return of the narcissist is that something that they wanted in their life is not going as planned. It could be that they are having a difficult time securing another victim. It could be that their new catch is not as submissive and willing to give the attention that the old victim gave. It could also do with not having to learn a whole other person's weaknesses as well as going through the entire process again with someone else.

It could very well just be a power game to show the victim that the narcissist is still in control. That they are able to manipulate the victim in any way that they want to use them and then discard them again at their whim. They are in no way in love with the victim other than for what the victim can offer.

The narcissists will put on a complete act along with crocodile tears if necessary to display the level of emotion they feel for hurting the victim. They are so good at this act, many victims believe them in their fragile state and want to comfort the narcissist.

The narcissist knows the best way to get them back is through their emotions because it is the easiest way to manipulate a victim who is just coming out of this state of being. The victim has not yet been able to healthily deal with the emotions that were felt during the relationship and are not in a place to make rational decisions.

And of course, when the victim hears something that they have been starved from for an extended amount of time, there is a psychological relief of finally getting recognition for the things they had experienced. When the narcissists profess their love or actually says sorry when they have not said it for months, it is difficult for anyone to not pay attention and be drawn in.

These masters of falsehoods may even make up stories of how they need the help of the victim. It could be something simple that the victim knows better or could be an elaborate cry for help because something dramatic or embarrassing happened. The narcissist makes the victim feel special because they say that no one other than the victim would understand or be able to help. In the end, it is the same story as a boy who cried wolf. This tactic can also be used as a way to drain the victim's time from their day.

Sometimes the narcissist will go to more extreme measures, especially if the love bombing and sorry phase do not make the victim come crawling back. They may start spreading nasty rumors about the victim to their friends, family members, coworkers or even perfect strangers. This tactic is known as a smear campaign and can even go as far to involve revenge porn.

The narcissist pulls out all the stops and lets their imagination run wild. They will come up with the most outrageous stories to defame and slander the victim where they are forced to stand up for themselves. The narcissist will even go as far as calling the victim a narcissist which brings the victim's supposed supporters to the side of the narcissist. This is also the point that the narcissist will bring up the embarrassing acts that the victim shamefully did during the relationship and bring them to the public eye.

The smear campaigns are quite effective in bringing further shame to the victim and furthering the isolation they most likely had felt during the relationship. Many times, this brings the victim back to the narcissist so that they can somehow prove to the narcissist that they are not that bad of a person and to clear their reputation.

However, the damage is already done. It is during the smut throwing that the victim finds out who their true friends and family members are as anyone who knows the real person, they would not believe any of this manipulative shaming.

This is an extremely hurtful and vulnerable position for the victim to be in, and the narcissist knows this. They are putting pressure on the victim to punish them for leaving, or they want them to feel like they are not able to function properly without them.

The narcissist has been manipulating you the entire time, so why would they stop now? This is a good phrase to memorize and ponder during the times that the narcissist seemed to have changed back to the person that you always loved and knew was deep down inside of them somewhere.

It is utterly important for the victim to block out the narcissist from their life if at all possible. Doing this will minimize the chance of them being drawn back in by the master manipulator. Know that even if the victim has not been in communication with their ex for a while, the moment they do, it can easily throw them back to the starting point.

When a victim is actively communicating with their ex, they are setting up their own dissolution. They are tearing themselves down and all the healing that they have gained since going no contact. The manipulator makes the victim think they must stand up for themselves, when in fact, the narcissist is gaining more power over the victim.

When a narcissist starts the cycle of wanting to return to a victim's life, this is to ensure that the victim is still feeling the pain that was caused during the relationship. It is a way to bring the victim back to ground zero and to the thick of it. This can even be done while stalking the victim or calling out of the blue after a long silence, just to instill the fear once again in the victim after they have hopefully moved on.

Just know that if the narcissist still sees you are something valuable, they will pull out any and every stop you could not even imagine. Because they have no filter for proper behavior towards another human being, there is no limit as to where they will stop if they want to be vindictive towards you or even to get you back.

The tactics they will use will have logical sense and are made to further make you feel like you are the crazy one that needs major help instead of the narcissist. This is a trap, and you must not fall for this. If you are able, the best way is to go no contact and start walking the other direction.

You will be thankful that you listened to your mind during this process instead of your heart as you will be playing tug of war between both until you chose a side.

FROM PARENTING TOGETHER TO CO-PARENTING APART

<u>Impact of Separation</u>

Loneliness after a divorce or separation can be frequent and even expected. You shared life with your spouse or partner, perhaps raising children and possibly planning a future together. Divorce and separations bring out strong emotions, many of which lead to feelings of loneliness.

What are the causes, and what can you do to manage loneliness after a divorce?

What Makes You Feel Lonely After A Divorce or Separation?

When a relationship ends, many factors can contribute to loneliness after separation:

- Pain, sadness, and anger: Divorce and separations can trigger an emotional turmoil. Emotions such as pain, grief, and even violence can be universal. They can lead you to distance yourself from other people and isolate yourself, which can lead to feelings of loneliness over time.

- Separation from family and friends: When a divorce or separation occurs, it is common to distance yourself from groups of friends and the family circle, especially those close to your ex. Those people were an essential part of your shared life and could completely disappear from your new life. And let's not forget about pets. Many divorces and separations also mean that a beloved family pet will go with one or the other. If you had a close relationship with a pet that is no longer there, this absent "loved one" could also make you feel lonely.

- Child Custody: When there are children involved in a divorce, there are generally custody issues that need to be addressed. If you share custody with a former partner, there may be times when you find yourself alone with no children around to distract you. It can also help you feel lonely after a divorce.

- Nostalgia for the holidays: Many couples and families have regular holiday traditions, usually shared with family and friends. Divorce and separations can change all of that. When those holidays get closer, they can bring with them a feeling of loneliness.

How Can You Handle Loneliness After A Relationship Ends?

- Accept your feelings of loneliness after a separation: You suddenly lost someone important in your life. It is not physically present, nor emotionally. You may also feel disconnected and removed from others. As you overcome the pain and heal of separation, you may experience periods of loneliness that can be a regular part of the process of moving on.

- Avoid having a relationship out of spite: Don't let the loneliness after your separation or divorce push you into another relationship too soon. If you are using a link out of spite to avoid loneliness or the emotions of a departure, you may need to reconsider. Instead, try spending a little time with yourself to recover before you start dating again.

- Join a support group for divorced people: You are not alone. Therapy groups offer the opportunity to gain help, understanding, and perspective from others who are going through a similar experience. Loneliness after a divorce is widespread, and you will likely find others in your same situation who are willing to speak, listen, and offer advice.

- Start a new routine: Losing a relationship can also mean that your lifestyle has changed dramatically. If you lived with your spouse or partner, you possibly had a daily routine. The longer that relationship or marriage has been, the more accustomed you would be to that daily routine. A separation can change all of that, and, as a result, you become disoriented and aimless. Methods such as feeding, sleeping, and even exercise routines are set aside, affecting your health and well-being. If you exercised regularly, do it again. Exercising can help stimulate endorphins, which could make you feel happier. So, tries to plan a new routine for yourself to see if it enables you to counteract some of the factors that contributed to loneliness after separation.

- Get Involved: Whether as a volunteer or joining a club, interacting with other people can stimulate endorphins in the brain two and help make you a happier person. Find volunteer options or clubs for people who share the same interests and stay open to new friends and support networks.

- Be kind to yourself: Find special activities that give you satisfaction. Try to enjoy some pleasant moments every day. Maybe you enjoy a walk, a foam bath, yoga, reading a good book, or listening to your favourite music. Whatever it is that brings you immediate happiness, spend time doing it. Developing good habits like these can help you manage the feeling of loneliness when you end a relationship.

How Long Can You Feel Lonely After A Divorce or Separation?

The length of feelings of loneliness after a divorce or separation depends on the factors you are dealing with the situation. The opinions of social isolation and disconnection from others may not be constant; a particular case can cause them, or they can appear and disappear. For example, holidays can bring periods of loneliness that then go.

For most people, loneliness after a divorce or separation is temporary and part of the grieving and healing process. If loneliness lingers and doesn't seem to end, it may be time to talk to your doctor, therapist, or other health care provider about chronic loneliness. They can help.

Impact on Children

It is essential to define some concepts to start our journey. Divorce is the act of dissolving or separating the marriage by sentence, with the effective cessation of conjugal coexistence or separating people who lived in a close relationship.

In Colombia, in the first seven months of 2016, the city with the most divorces reported by the Superintendence of Notaries and Registry was Bogotá with 2,923, followed by Cali with 1,238 and thirdly Medellín with 824.

Among the most frequent causes of divorce, infidelity is reported first, followed by financial problems, then the lack of balance in the time spent in the family, marital violence, and the lack of definition in the execution of the work. Domestic.

A divorce is then an event that occurs within the dynamics of the couple, which is a large percentage of families that do not happen at any given time but is part of a sequence of conflicts in which children are immersed both actively as passive.

Divorce Is Characterized by Three Stages

- Pre divorce stage: in turn, composed of two sub-phases, the phase of manifest conflict: in which the typical problems of the couple's life are maximized. There is dissatisfaction, discomfort, disappointment, emotional and physical withdrawal begins, but they may exist reconquest attempts. Then comes the second phase of emotional divorce, in which the positive effects are overridden by the negative ones, and a series of verbal and physical confrontations and attacks begin, in which attempts are made to place the children against the other parent.

- Trans divorce stage: legal, economic divorce and problems of custody and parental relationship begin, where on many occasions, the benefit of the children does not matter, which are used in the conflict trying to "earn them" through emotional blackmail, gifts, and privileges.

- Post-divorce stage: social or community divorce is involved, there is a conflict of loyalties in the children. But, at the same time, it is a critical stage because the preparation of mourning begins. There are new friendships and routines with the children, and a final psychological elaboration phase, with acceptance of the loss.

THE EFFECTS OF DIVORCE

Depending on gender, children have different reactions to this event.

Children seem to have more significant difficulties in going through the crisis, in the intensity of their feelings and their duration. It is more frequent than they present more school problems than the girls, becoming much more irritable, and that some violent behaviors appear.

As for the girls, they will show their feelings with less violence, and they tend to withdraw and speak little; on some occasions, they become anxious or, on the contrary, they behave excessively well and present a better social, school, and emotional development.

In addition to gender differences, we have different ways of assuming parents' divorce according to age. In the first year of life, children do not understand the concept of separation but begin to notice changes in the environment, in the caregiver and routines.

Regarding development, in the stage of essential confidence vs Basic mistrust, which is why in this phase. The child must be given appropriate support, and their basic needs must be met by their caregivers, to stimulate the development of confidence. If this accompaniment is not provided, it can manifest itself as an insecure attachment, with whims, irritability, sadness, changes in sleep and appetite patterns, and delay in meeting developmental milestones, constituting a response to maternal stress and depression.

Between 1 and 2 years, according to Erikson, the stage of autonomy vs shame and doubt. May manifest with excessive crying, difficulty being away from the mother, even for a moment. It is why she can use maternal substitutes, such as blankets and stuffed animals, and will also have difficulty sleeping or staying asleep.

From 3 to 5 years old, the stage of autonomy vs shame and doubt and the start of the initiative stage vs guilt. It could manifest as regressions to achievements obtained in previous stages of development, possessiveness, excessively good behavior, and on some occasions, aggressiveness.

In schoolchildren, those who go through the industry stage vs inferiority. There are more significant cognitive growth and a better understanding of the concept and the permanence of divorce. There may be a decrease in school performance. Also, they can develop feelings of loss, rejection, and guilt. There is a conflict of loyalties concerning their parents, for which they present concern about losing the father who does not live with them and being replaced, propensity to blame themselves for the dissolution of the marriage of their parents and even may develop reunion fantasies.

Adolescents are in the identity vs stage. Diffusion of identity; They may feel very anxious, highly concerned about their future, or present intense anger, in addition to outsourcing problems that can lead to drug, alcohol, and even rule violations.

Strategies to Improve Coping

We will focus on strategy according to the age and stage of development that the child is going through.

In infants, we must ensure early secure attachment with a trusted caregiver, consistency in routines, increased interaction time with primary caregivers, and reinforce positive social interactions.

In preschoolers, we must continue with consistency in routines; the child must have quality time with her parents, and they must understand that the child is full of doubts. So, she will ask repetitive questions that will help her in the processing of the information; Besides, your caregivers must provide accurate and appropriate information about the divorce process and explain that it will affect daily life.

The students need reminders that the divorce is final and that they are not to blame because at this stage tend to blame themselves for the separation of their parents. Additionally, they must maintain relationships with both parents, who must allow them to express their feelings openly.

As for teens, it is important to have quiet conversations about the reaction to divorce, and teens should not be held accountable for legal and financial issues, which should be apparent from the start; They may also need individual or group therapy.

Recommendations for Pediatricians

Pediatricians should spend time talking to the child alone during consultations, at the beginning and during the divorce, and after the process.

Dialogue with parents so as not to involve the child in the conflict; Besides, they should talk to them about essential sources of support.

The pediatrician should avoid taking sides or identifying with one parent and going against the other.

Bear in mind the possibility of suspected abuse or neglect and always make the proper notification.

Determine according to each case if the support of any other specialist is needed.

Recommendations for Parents

Always be careful with what they say and how they say it. Find the best way to tell children that parents separate; ideally, both parents should be present at that time. How you want to communicate it to the child will depend on the age, sometimes the use of drawings or stories can be useful.

Clarify to the children that they are not responsible for the separation and that it is not in their hands to recompose the marriage. Reaffirm that both parents will continue to love them the same after the separation.

Talk to all the children at the same time, regardless of whether they are of different ages, this way they can help each other. Prepare answers to the following questions: Who am I going to live with between my parents? Will I have to move?

Clearly explain what will and will not change in your life. Avoid putting children as spies, messengers, or judges, and don't argue in front of them. Assure the child that he will be visited by the father who does not live with him and fulfil his promises.

Ensure that the visits are pleasant and that the child expresses when he gets home how well he spent with the other parent.

Conclusions

A divorce is an event within the couple dynamics in which conflicts occur; the children are going to be immersed. Children's feelings dissolution of the couple may be expressed in different ways, age the stage of development in they are. It must be taken into account early to intervene if necessary.

Children must always be accompanied in this process, clearly explaining what is happening and the changes that will come. Clarify to the children that they are not guilty of the moment the couple is going through and that it is not their function or their duty to unite their parents again. Children and their parents must have regular support and observations from health personnel.

<u>Co-parenting Goals</u>

One of the most challenging things for parents is to tell the children that father and mother are separating. Since this is a significant cut in children's lives, they should only be discussed with them once the separation has been firmly and finally decided. Parents' considerations as to whether a separation or divorce should take

74

place with the children should never be discussed with the children. It would only unnecessarily burden the children, who, depending on their age, for example, because of school or puberty. Conversely, it should still be talked about a decided separation that is again delayed (for example, because one parent is always looking for a flat). Because the children inevitably notice when the parents are distant due to the final and upcoming separation. Here the children should not be left in the dark and thereby disturbed, but specific conditions created are.

Another question is how to convey to the later children of divorce that the parents no longer love each other. Only younger schoolchildren who go to primary school can understand from their thinking that the parents no longer understand each other and therefore have the opportunity to separate. It is much more difficult for smaller children. If they were told, for example, that the separation was due to constant arguments, the answer from their way of thinking would be rough: "But why then, I also quarreled with Linda from kindergarten and now we're friends again." Smaller children are therefore best told that father and mother no longer want to live together and that everyone wants to live their own life.

The reasons for the separation disputes should depend on age, be explained to the children briefly and only in a few sentences. Detailed justifications should be avoided since they regularly contain "adult issues" with which the children are entirely overwhelmed. In a way, this applies to adolescents who, because of puberty, are primarily concerned with cutting off parents and developing personalities. Conflicts of loyalty among children should be avoided at all costs to evoke. If, for example, one parent was left because the other had fallen in love with a new partner, the children would quickly say: "Papa doesn't want to live with me anymore, he fell in love with another woman." It awakens the feeling of the children that they have to stick to the abandoned parent and should no longer love the other one. Responsible parents should spare their children with this emotional balancing act.

CHILDREN WANT TO KNOW HOW TO PROCEED

Once the children understand that the parents are separating, especially smaller children and younger school children ask very pragmatic questions. These are, for example: "Where do I sleep (if we move out)?", "Is there enough space for my toys?" Or "Who will drive me to kindergarten?" Parents talk to children for the first time about the decided separation should have thought of an answer to all questions in advance. It also presupposes that the parents have at least roughly agreed on what future togetherness with the children should look. Also, the children should be involved in all questions relating to the future. If the mother is looking for a new apartment for herself and the children, she can Take children to the viewing appointment and say that these could be your rooms, and so we could furnish the apartment. If the new studio is renovated itself, the children can help. In this way, the children know how to proceed and

experience a certain amount of security that takes away their fear.

HOW PARENTS SHOULD DEAL WITH IT

Children have significant problems when the father and mother finally separate. When one parent moves out, the previous world collapses for future children of divorces. From the perspective of the children, the family's security ceases to exist, they are initially completely disoriented and first have to learn to deal with the new situation. Even if every child reacts differently: Almost every child shows specific age-typical reactions, whereby the transitions are fluid.

- Babies and toddlers also notice when a parent moves out and thus separates with the toddler. The helplessness of the children often shows up in tantrums and aggressive behavior. Others are afraid and do not leave the remaining parent alone for a moment. Because according to the children's thinking, this parent could also leave them. Finally, some children go backwards: they wet themselves again or want the pacifier back; all of this was already a thing of the past. The parent with whom the babies and toddlers live should have patience and be there for the children despite their separation problems. Regular contacts or visits to the parent who has moved out should take place, even if only for a few hours. The children's fear of loss can be gradually reduced. It will take some time until the future children of divorce have security again, especially since there is no sense of time yet.

- Children of kindergarten age react in a similar way to babies and toddlers, albeit much more clearly. So, it can happen that they beat other children in the daycare centre, not lunch, eat like it, or refuse to go to the toilet. At this age, they are not aware that other people can perceive the world differently than they. Relationship and affection are developed through concrete "doing something together," in which the children see themselves as the focus. If a parent is less available due to move out, the children perceive as a love deprivation due to way of thinking. The children look for the reasons for this and believe that they are to blame for the separation.

- A typical example of this is that a child tends to tidy up his room after a long time, which he never did despite the parents' ranting, and now thinks: "Now I've cleaned up, my parents don't need to argue about me anymore. " Clear structures and relative orientation of what will be in the future are essential for children of kindergarten age. Both parents - especially the one with whom the children live - are required to give the children security and fear despite the separation. The reliability of the parents is the top priority here. Also, everything that is important for the children should be integrated into the new ways of life of the parents and the people to whom the children have a fixed relationship.

- When the children go to primary school, they can already partially understand what is happening in the family and how they are separated from children. The later children of divorce recognize that other people perceive the world differently than they do. The children think, however, that the others are expressing their actual intentions through their actions. The children cannot yet recognize the hidden intentions of other people. For the first time, children can understand the changes affecting them themselves through the separation of parents, as well as express feelings such as sadness and the desire for the parent to return. Even so, the children are helpless, sad, and angry. Sometimes school performance deteriorates and dealing with friends and classmates suffer. Also, there are the first conflicts of loyalty.

- On the one hand, some children would like to assist the "abandoned," "lonelier" parent who needs support, for example, by doing household chores. On the other hand, the children themselves need help from what they believe is the healthier parent. Most of the time, the children, therefore, want the parents to get together again, and there is no divorce with the children - which expresses the children's desire to avoid the conflict of loyalty. Parents need to be aware of this phase of their children. The parent grieving for the end of the relationship should not continuously burden the children with their problems. But the parent who ended the association should also handle it sensitively in the presence of the children. A piece of normality in the changed living conditions is desirable here. Also, recently, schooled children need a large part of their strength and energy to find their way in the new environment they are unfamiliar with. Parents should also take this into account when separating children.

- Older schoolchildren up to around 12 years of age recognize that the actions and intentions of other people can fall apart, whereby behind "unpleasant" effects can also be good intentions. Love and closeness between children and parents are no longer shaped by action, but by mutual feelings. It means concern for the well-being of others, combined with the recognition of goodwill. If the child recognizes the good intentions and beliefs of the parents, positive emotions are evoked. Conversely, there can now also be conflicts between children and parents come because of different attitudes and opinions - and no longer exclusively because of behavior that is perceived as unpleasant. Due to development, there may be strong solidarity between the children and one parent due to the separation or divorce. The children ally with the parent injured by the separation and sometimes even assume the role of the missing partner, which the parent unconsciously accepts. It inevitably leads to alienation from the other parent. If this is recognized by the parent with whom the children ally, they can be manipulated extremely (so-called Parental Alienation Syndrome- PAS). Unfortunately, there are always cases in practice in which mothers abandoned by their husbands influence the children against the father in this way, which sometimes leads to the children breaking off contact. Other possible reactions from children of this age are that they lose all respect due to the constant arguments between parents about them. Because the parents fail their authority over the children, massive educational problems often arise. Again, the children should not be burdened too much with parental difficulties. The separation, the children, need the support of parents, in turn, have to seek help other than children because of problems. Also, the function of partner replacement overwhelms the children in the long run, since they deal with conflicts that are not age-appropriate. Due to the associated impairment of the ability to concentrate, the children's performance can drop. The future children of divorce must have fun in life, at school, in hobbies, with friends, with the support of their parents, so that in the event of separation despite having a child, they can again approach both parents with ease and joy.

- At the latest from around 15 years of age, the children can view things in a higher-level way, that is, to see and generalize their point of view and that of others from a "third person's point of view." At the same time, due to puberty, the children are busy separating from their parents and developing into their personality. Conversely, parents often seek consolation and support from their children because of the separation, which disrupts their development. The results sometimes very violent reactions from young people, ranging from "zero bocks" to drug or alcohol consumption to the search for support from friends. However, some young people also take sides with a parent and are almost hostile to the other. And some young people want to have contact with both parents but are afraid that this will injure the "weaker" parent. If adolescents are older, it can also happen that they completely withdraw from the home where they want to move out or flee to friends. As a result, separation with children often leads to adolescents growing up faster than is right for them. One of the biggest problems for young people, when their parents are separated, is that the general support breaks down in the awkward phase of personal development. Even though adolescents are "rebellious" during puberty and often behave negatively towards their parents, they know that the parents are ultimately there for them. Despite the separation, the parents should therefore clearly reduce their problems vis-à-vis the young people. Young people are allowed to have their own experiences. However, the parents should convey to their children that they are there for them despite the separation with help and advice, if the young people want it. This Support should be offered to children even if they misbehave towards their parents. At the same time, clear rules are essential.

Ideally, the parents talk about this and exchange ideas about the jointly observed development of adolescents.

These Are the Legal Conditions for Separation with Children

After the separation, other questions related to children are essential. It includes custody, the right to determine residence, the power of access, the right to information about the personal circumstances of the child, and maintenance for the children. In the context of the child, subsistence is regulated, the parent receives the child support in separation or the child support in a divorce.

Both Parents Have Custody

If the parents were married to each other (or have each issued declarations of care for the children), they have joint custody of the children, Section 1626 of the German Civil Code (BGB). It also applies to the period after separation or divorce.

A total of three areas of shared parental care in separation and divorce can be distinguished, § 1687 BGB:

- The decisions in matters of everyday life are made by the parent with whom the child is habitually resident. These include decisions about school tuition, the treatment of minor illnesses, or the specific stay with relatives.

- In matters of actual childcare, the parent who is authorized to handle decides when the child is with him. It includes the type of diet or bedtime.

- Decisions on matters of significant importance can only be made by parents together. Such choices include the choice of school or vocational training, approval of operations (except in urgent cases), or fundamental decisions about where to live.

- A parent receives sole custody only if this is applied for at the family court. Child welfare is crucial. Only if this is endangered or impaired, can the court wholly or partially withdraw parental responsibility, § 1666 BGB? For example, there are dangers or impairments to the child's well-being if the children are at risk of being neglected or if urgently required healing treatments are not given. Another case that can lead to a complete deprivation of custody is the parents' unwillingness to communicate. For example, if the parents stop talking to each other after a bitter divorce war, this can lead to the custody of the person with whom the children of divorce are not habitually resident.

Right of Residence for Divorced Children

The question of whom the children should live with after the separation is of considerable importance in practice. For this purpose, the parents as an outflow of personal care - must agree on whom the child should have his permanent residence with, 1627 BGB. If this is not possible, the family court decides on the right of residence, § 1628 BGB. However, custody and power of residence determination must be separated. For example, the mother may have the right to determine home, but both parents have care.

Right of Access: The Parents Are Obliged and Entitled

The child has the right to deal with each parent, whereby each parent is obliged and entitled to deal with the child, Section 1684 (1) BGB. The child has its right to deal with parents, from which the parents can, in turn, derive their power to deal with the child. Conversely, the parent who is entitled to access should not forego dealing with the child for reasons of child welfare.

So that the handling is not impaired, the so-called ethical conduct clause applies to both parents according to § 1684 (2) BGB. According to regulation, parents "must refrain from, which affects the relationship of the child to the other parent or complicates the upbringing." It means that the parents are mutually prohibited from negatively influencing the child compared to the other parent. Also, grandparents, siblings, step-parents, and other vital caregivers have a right to deal with the children of divorce if this serves the child's best interests, Section 1685 (1) and (2) BGB.

If there are disputes about the handling or if this should be restricted or excluded for reasons of child welfare, the family court decides, §§ 1684 Abs. 3, 1685 Abs. 3 BGB. It also includes the cases in which the court orders "accompanied" ("sheltered") handling in the presence of a willing third party (e.g., from the German Child Protection Association) to rule out a risk to the well-being of the child or to initiate initial contact between father and child.

The Children Can Have A Say

Depending on how old they are, the children are allowed to have a say in custody, the determination of residence, and handling. For example, when dealing with the wish of even a six- to the seven-year-old child, the family court must take into account. For example, the withdrawal of custody from a parent against the will of a 14-year-old child is almost impossible. To exercise their rights, the children also receive from the court a method counsel assigned (known lawyer of the child), § 158 Act on Proceedings in Family Matters and Matters of Voluntary Jurisdiction (FamFG).

In practice, however, it is difficult for young children, especially small children, to have a permanent stay with the father, if the father works full-time while the mother is a housewife.

The Right to Information About the Circumstances of The Child

In practice, the right to information about the child's circumstances is rarely used following § 1686 BGB. The judicial officer decides on this claim, which is treated somewhat "neglected" by some family courts. According to this, the parents are obliged, if there is a legitimate interest, to provide the other parent with information about the child's circumstances unless this contradicts the best interests of the child.

This claim is significant if, for example, one of the parents has no dealings with the child. Here, this parent can request - usually every six months - two photos of the child, a copy of the school report, and a report on the development, interests, and health status of the child. It does not matter that the child does not want this information to be released. The claim is only excluded if there is a risk that this information will be misused.

Children Are Entitled to Maintenance

Maintenance is one of the questions that need to be dealt with when separating children or divorcing children.

Where to Find Help and Advice on Out-of-court Conflict Resolution

Even if many parents are willing to compromise after separation for the benefit of the children, a friendly solution cannot always be found. The local youth welfare offices offer help and advice, and they also provide information on the advice provided by other local bodies and institutions.

If no agreement is reached in this way either, the only option left is the way to the family court. Since laypersons cannot understand the matter, it makes sense to consult a specialist lawyer for family law. In difficult financial circumstances, legal aid can obtain. The lawyer will also be happy to advise you on this.

Core Concepts of Positive Parenting

The positive parenting style is a parenting style that is based on respect for children, raised with love, and, above all, doing so through non-violent behavior. Currently, there is a will of many parents for non-violent parenting. Still, on many occasions, parents need support, advice, and tools to manage the challenges and conflicts of family life daily in a positive and non-positive way. Violent.

What Is Positive Parenting and What Is It?

It is not easy to find a definition of positive parenting. Still, it does not matter the language in which it is spoken or where you are. In positive parenting, you work with the same objectives, and parents share a shared vision: use affection as a basis of education.

Positive parenting fosters the relationship between parents and children based on mutual respect, helping children to develop properly, and children to grow up so that they know how to relate to others in a non-violent and constructive way.

It is important to praise good behavior, setting clear rules, really listening to children, working as a team, and of course, using positive discipline instead of physical or psychological punishment.

Therefore, positive parenting is parenting that recognizes children as individuals with rights that must be respected.

How to Get Positive Parenting at Home?

Although below you will read some tips to achieve a positive upbringing at home, you must remember that it is a lifestyle, beliefs that must be had and respected in the family, and above all, you will have to forget about negative discipline in your home.

- Be a good example. Children need the case of their parents. If your child witnesses loving and respectful relationships at home, they will be more likely to adopt those same values.

- Understand your child's personality. Every child is dissimilar and may need unlike kinds of guidance to suit their personality. For example, a very active and stubborn child will need a different approach to positive discipline than a calmer and more reserved child.

- Think about the needs behind the behavior. If your child is jumping on the couch, it is because he will need to burn energy or maybe because you have been working too hard, and he wants to get your attention or simply because he is bored.

- Help your child express his feelings. Communication needs to work in a family that everyone knows and is taught to express feelings and also to share them before they are challenging to control.

Parenting Guidelines

Parenting as an educational process aims to guide children and adolescents to live well in the adventure of life, through intelligent and affectionate accompaniment by parents or significant adults.

The parenting guidelines are not recipes with which a good child is prepared, and they are diverse according to the culture, the family trait, the social content. Despite this, here are some that should be taken into account:

- Know and assume the rights of children and adolescents as responsibilities that adults have to guarantee their sound development.

- The masculine presence is essential in the development of the children and the family coexistence. Therefore, it is not only the mother's task to educate and raise.

- The proper treatment is having joy, availability of time and space to share with the children and the couple, the game, the care, the accompaniment in work, and the strengthening of the emotional bond. It implies maintaining excellent communication and respect for the other from the difference, establishing agreements in the couple in terms of authority mediated by dialogue.

- Accompaniment at different stages of development, a 6-month-old baby is not the same as a 6-year-old, each has different needs; each step of the child is important and deserves attention and stimulation.

- Use the game as a learning tool where it is possible to develop a recreational way to feed the spirit, improve other functions, exercise the body, and finally be happy. Play should be a way of implementing values and generating creativity.

- Authority, rather than a way of giving orders, is expressing discipline with love. For them, the couple must establish clear rules since the child is young. When the norm is not complied with, create dialogue and define if it deserves a sanction, if this happens, it must be met, each time we give up oblivion and remain in the promise, we subtract points from the authority. In the same way that a sanction is applied, it is essential to establish recognition for the right actions. In creating power, it is necessary to forget that this traumatized the child, and that will be the way to achieve obedience in the other person.

Growth Development Goals

The upbringing in itself must bet to some development goals, that is to say, to some purposes that facilitate the effectiveness of the achievements and become a motivating force, these are:

- Self-esteem: judgment about oneself, is the ability to consider being capable of doing. The concept of self-esteem is mediated by self-recognition (recognizing corporality and the use of tools), self-concept (ideas around body parts) and self-definition (who thinks of himself in terms of virtue, competence, and power)

- Autonomy: Ability to develop and determine one's will against the norm.

- Creativity is the ability to create in the personal, the familiar, the artistic, the scientific, and the social, achieving superior well-being.

- Happiness: state of vital affirmation, the ability to make plans, or choices that are enjoyed.

- Solidarity: it is the promotion of the collective before any particular consideration; it is giving confidence.

- Health: it is the complete physical, mental and social well-being, and not only the absence of the disease.

- Resilience is the ability to cope after or during failure.

COMMUNICATION PROTOCOLS

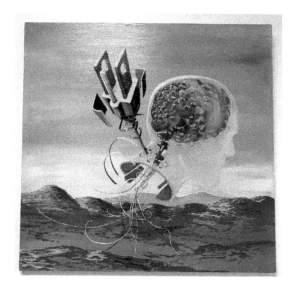

Modes of Communication

Let's face it: communicating with an ex-husband, ex-wife, or ex-partner is not always easy. Talking is often easier said than done. Feelings like anger, confusion, or nerves can make it difficult to say what you want or need to say. Although your relationship may have ended, communicating with a former spouse or former partner may be necessary on occasions such as when children are involved. By doing the good of giving your children a happier and healthier childhood with both parents involved, applying effective communication techniques to your conversations with your ex will be of benefit to you.

The constructive modules of effective communication after divorce begin with a commitment to raising your children together and creating the best possible environment for them to thrive. Remembering your commitment to them can help you and your former partner to continue a goal for what you hope to accomplish in your parenting collaboration. With your focus always in mind, you can turn your attention to creating different modules of effective communication.

Language

Effective communication depends mostly on the choice of language and words. Saying the wrong things in converison at the wrong time can quickly change the course to where you would not have wished to have chosen. Sometimes the words can be misinterpreted, and the listener can give it a different meaning. So, it is essential to choose wisely. Choose the appropriate words to convey what you need to say adequately. Avoid language that has no other function than to hurt the other person. It may include an insult or different vulgar language.

<u>Way of talking</u>

Like word choice, how those words are conveyed is as essential to building effective communication. Your method of transmission, tone of voice, and timing are all aspects to consider when communicating. Choose a manner that allows you to deliver your message accurately. Depending on what you are talking about and how well you communicate verbally with your ex-spouse or ex-partner, face-to-face or over the phone conversations may not always be the best way to transmit individual messages. Written communication may work best for some former couples since it allows long-distance conversation. It can give you the confidence to convey what you want to say more clearly. Even when written communication is used as your preferred method of communication, the tone still carries a lot of weight. The sound in written communication is not entirely based on the choice of words. Punctuations express volume, the use of capital letters, quotation marks, underlining. Other punctuation marks can change the tone of your written voice in a way that perhaps did not intend to do so. Avoid excessive use of dramatic punctuation. Finally, time can have a significant impact on how a person receives a message. While negotiating a parenting time exchange, it is probably not the time to touch on sensitive issues with your ex-spouse or ex-partner. Keep the more severe conversations reserved for times when you and your ex-partner can adequately focus on the issue at hand without putting your children in the middle of the conflict.

Listening

There are moments to speak, and there are moments to listen. It is often true that the moments of listening are just as, if not more, crucial to building effective communication after divorce. When I don't hear what the other person had to say correctly, how am I supposed to make a proper response? Be attentive during conversations with your former spouse or partner, listening carefully, or thoroughly reading the messages you receive. Don't jump to reply, take a moment to understand what you've heard, and then write your reply. If you don't know what to say or feel like you're about to explode, it's okay to say you need to talk about this later. However, don't forget the conversation, come back to it when you once feel

ready to focus and give a smooth and effective response.

CONCLUSION

Thank you for reading all this book!

If you still aren't sure about making this change, sit down and really look at how your life has been trying to "help" the other person. When was the last time that you did something for yourself? This is the most important thing that you can do if you are still questioning things. You've probably not really looked at your life from a perspective other than the other person. Once you do this, you'll start to realize that changes must be made.

Once you are ready to make those changes, sit down and come up with an action plan. Depending on your relationship with the other person, this action plan can vary. This is where it can get tricky or hard, but this is also where you should find somebody that you trust that can help you to get out of the relationship.

You have already taken a step towards your improvement.

Best wishes!

CPSIA information can be obtained
at www.ICGtesting.com
Printed in the USA
BVHW051554130421
604814BV00004B/924

9 781802 235098